WALKING WITH
JAMES

Becoming The Man God Intended You To Be

A 30-DAY DEVOTIONAL
AND BIBLE STUDY

FRED J. PARRY

Walking With James
Becoming The Man God Intended You To Be
A 30-day Devotional and Bible Study

ISBN: 9781642541847

Interior Design: Carolyn Preul
Copy Editing: Sandy Selby and Lisa Thornton Stillwell
Technical Review: Bob Walz and Larry Glabe

Printed in the United States of America

For Melody, Max and Nick

*In reconciliation for those many times I fell short
of being the man God intended me to be.*

CONTENTS

For more information on using this book for a group study, please visit **www.FredParry.Life** for study materials, handouts, and other useful information.

PREFACE

Everything I needed to know in life, I could have learned from reading the Book of James!

As odd as it may seem, that statement is absolutely true. As a man, I've grown accustomed to learning life's lessons the hard way. Looking back, I realize I could have avoided a lot of rough patches if I had discovered the wisdom of the Book of James when I was a younger man … but I didn't open a Bible until I was 42. By that time, I had made just about every stupid mistake known to man.

If I had known about James's lessons on humility, patience and controlling my temper, it would have made me a better father and a more loving husband. If I had discovered his advice about worry, compassion, and pride, it would have made me an altogether better human being. Instead, like so many other men, I got caught up in life's rat race, trying to stay on top and in control.

If I had studied what James had to say about persistence, complacency and dealing with life's challenges, I would have been a more successful businessman. I could have avoided all those late nights and weekends spent at the office neglecting my job as a husband and father. I could have dodged the angst, anxiety, and frustration that come with running a business and managing employees. I might have been a person my colleagues admired instead of a person they dreaded. Looking back, I have many regrets, but now, thanks to the lessons from this wonderful book in the Bible, I have renewed hope as I move forward with a greater sense of peace and understanding.

You, too, may be surprised to discover so many life-changing pearls of wisdom in one of the shortest books in the Bible.

My goal in creating this 30-day devotional and Bible study is to give men of all ages and walks of life a better chance to know what it means to live life as a real Christian. It all starts with words of wisdom from James, the real-life half-brother of Jesus Christ. The subtitle of this book "Becoming The Man God Intended You To Be" may be a bit of a misnomer in that it sets up the expectation for a remarkably fast transformation. My hope is that you'll take the time to ponder the ideas presented by James and consider how they might apply to your life. My guess is that you'll be surprised at the comprehensive scope and breadth of this guide to Christian living.

When I began my faith journey in 2006, a mentor suggested spending 15 minutes each day reading the Bible. After making excuse after excuse for why I couldn't take the time, I finally conceded. The next step was particularly difficult; I didn't know where to start. That same friend recommended the Book of James, probably because he knew it was only five chapters long and even with my challenged attention span, there was a fighting chance I would actually read it from start to finish. Little did either of us know, his recommendation would open up a whole new world to me.

At first, it was like drinking from a firehose. I didn't understand the meaning or context for much of what I was reading, but the parts that were soaking in were compelling and inspiring. I had begun a new journey with Christ, but I knew I still had a lot of work to do. In the Book of James, I was finding little nuggets of wisdom that I could apply to almost every area of my troubled life. To increase my reading comprehension, I found it beneficial to go back and read the chapters more than once. Each time I read one of these short chapters, I was finding new meaning and encouragement. My understanding grew exponentially when I eventually sat down and discussed each line and verse with a small group of trusted friends.

The change that took place within me was significant. Up to that point in my life, I had become comfortable in my life of sin, doing things my own way, on my schedule and by my own set of rules. I would have been headed for disaster if not for the grace of God. My exposure to the Book of James was the first step in my journey and to finding meaning in my life. By spending time in the Word each day, I was beginning to better understand God's nature. It was an eye-opening experience to learn of His grace and mercy and His unconditional love for me. I found it ironic that while I had struggled to have a harmonious relationship with my earthly father, I was suddenly exploring the possibilities of a remarkable, personal relationship with my heavenly father.

A few years ago, I took a leap of faith and decided to host my own Friday morning Bible study with a group of 30 men. And yes, we chose the Book of James for our first study. I wanted other men to experience the sage wisdom that came from James. Unlike other parts of the Bible, the Book of James seemed easier to understand and digest. Through James's matter-of-fact, no-nonsense approach to Christian living, the guys in my group were able to receive God's word at face value, and we began to see lives and whole families being transformed, all because fathers and husbands were getting clarity about the lives that God intended them to live.

My Christian journey has been far from perfect. For every two steps I take forward, it seems I find myself taking a step back toward my sinful life. I guess that's why they call it a journey. I still suffer from a sense of brokenness and the wounds that come from having a distant father, a strong-willed mother, and painfully low self-esteem. Like a lot of men, I will occasionally return to those periods of isolation where I stubbornly insist on doing things my way and on my own. I now recognize that these temporary lapses are a breeding ground for sin and personal failure. As men, we were designed by God to find our way together, not on our own. Proverbs 27:17 says, "As iron sharpens iron, so one man sharpens another." We need other men in our lives to hold us accountable and to ask us the tough questions that we won't dare ask ourselves.

For that reason, this book is ideal for use in a group study. Even if it's just one other guy, I want to encourage you to share this experience with someone with whom you can be vulnerable and transparent. I believe the wisdom that comes from the Book of James can be transformational if we push ourselves to be authentic with one another. Because we all fall short of God's glory, we must be merciful with one another, extending the type of grace and understanding that God has so generously given each of us.

Finally, I want to stress the importance of keeping it "real" as you go through this study. Many of us will struggle with the themes presented in these chapters, and there should be no reluctance to reveal your fears, shame, and disappointment as you candidly discuss each topic. I admit there were times when I felt hypocritical writing some of these devotions. I still struggle in many of these areas and often fall miles short of God's expectations. I can, however, take comfort in knowing that I'm a work-in-progress. Even though I am far from being the type of man that God intended, I know that I'm growing closer to Him every day, and perhaps that should be the overriding goal. God has accepted me with all of my warts, bruises, and brokenness. I'm confident that He'll do the same for you.

— Fred J. Parry

God, thank you for Your abundant grace and for the wisdom You are sharing through the words of James. Grant me the courage to approach this study with an open heart and an authentic spirit. Give me the clarity of mind and the thirst for knowledge to discover what it takes to be the man You intend me to be. For these things and so much more, I pray in the name of Your son and our savior, Jesus Christ. Amen.

HOW TO USE THIS BOOK

Walking with James is designed to serve the dual purpose of being a daily devotional and a Bible study guide for the Book of James. While the book is structured to be used over 30 days, I would encourage you to use it at a pace that is most comfortable for you.

Each of the daily devotionals is inspired by one of the many pearls of wisdom found in the Book of James. These devotionals were written as responses from my own personal understanding of how a particular verse spoke to me. I'm confident that 100 different people could read the same verse and come up with at least 100 different applications. The goal of any Bible Study is to find the correct interpretation which leads to a variety of applications. That, in itself, is rightly handling the word of truth (2 Timothy 2:15).

If you're like me, you'll get a new insight or meaning each time you read one of these chapters and not because the Bible's meaning has changed, but because we, as individuals, change. We've become more aware of a different aspect of our lives, and this Scripture now speaks to us in a new way. We are more teachable than we were before. The Bible takes us on where we are, and God uses His Word to lead us to greater maturity and a broader perspective. The Bible is as deep as we are, and deeper still.

I would suggest approaching each devotional in prayer, asking God for clarity of mind and focus with a hope that the day's message resonates with you in some meaningful way. Once you've read the devotional, you'll find a reference to scripture outside the Book of James that will reinforce and add context to that day's message. Next, you'll spend a few minutes responding to the message by answering two short questions designed to help you apply that day's lesson to your life. Finally, you'll find the Contemplate section, which is intended as a prompt for journaling or to challenge deeper thinking. It's an excellent opportunity to explore your feelings as they relate to the day's message.

As the author of this study, it's important for me to point out that I am not a moral authority on the lessons of James or on any other topic. In the grand scheme of things, I am still somewhat immature in my Christian walk, and I'm simply desiring to grow closer to God by seeing this project through from start to finish. I wanted to create a Bible Study that was approachable to men, especially those who are just beginning their exploration of a personal relationship with Jesus Christ. Some will inevitably find this approach to be overly simplistic with many redundancies. Others will find sincere inspiration and will appreciate the frequent reinforcement of key ideals proposed by James for those desiring to live a more Christ-centered life.

— Fred J. Parry

WHO WAS JAMES?

The author of the epistle who inspired this study is James, the younger half-brother of Jesus, and also known as James the Just. After the death of Jesus, James became a leader in the early Christian church, eventually becoming the first bishop of Jerusalem.

James grew up in Nazareth, where he was the oldest of four sons born to Joseph and Mary, who were descendants of the Israelite tribe of Judah. Because Joseph was not the biological father of Jesus, James was the half-brother of Jesus. James's other brothers were named Joses, Simon, and Judas. Some Bible historians say there is evidence that at least two daughters were also born to Mary and Joseph.

It is recorded that James and his brothers showed little respect for Jesus during their childhood. They were reportedly concerned about their half-brother's peculiar behavior. They did not believe that Jesus was the Son of God or the Messiah (Mark 3:21). It wasn't until Jesus' death and subsequent resurrection that James and his brothers became believers. Shortly following his resurrection, Jesus appeared to James. This was a defining moment for James, and he quickly became a believer. From that point forward, he was completely committed to God. In addition to his early influence on the Christian church, James became an important mentor and advisor to the Apostle Paul.

Biblical scholars note that James was completely humbled by his relationship to Jesus and typically referred to himself only as a servant of Jesus, never making reference to the fact that Jesus was his half-brother. Because of his extraordinary virtue, he was frequently referred to as James the Just.

The Book of James is one of 21 epistles in the New Testament. It is a letter written to Jewish Christians who had scattered across the region to escape persecution. Even though James is one of the shortest books of the Bible, with just five chapters, it is perhaps the most often quoted. In fact, many scholars refer to the Book of James as the "Proverbs of the New Testament" because of the practical wisdom it shares with readers about growing their faith as obedient Christians. Of the 108 verses in the entire book, 60 are direct obligations that challenge Christians to apply the teachings of Jesus to their lives. Many believe James's epistle is written in a vein similar to Jesus's Sermon on the Mount (Matthew 5-7) because of its candid instructions regarding one's walk of faith.

In his writings, James emphasized the very fundamental tenets of what it meant to be a true Christian. The Epistle of James is filled with advice for Christian living, placing a strong emphasis on the virtues of patience and self-control. James emphasized the importance of seeking God's wisdom and gave encouragement for building a strong moral character. He wrote of the obligation to uphold the totality of God's laws (the Ten Commandments or Royal Law) and the overarching need for obedience. James strongly believed that the human heart too often longed for things that man should not have, so his writings were directed toward giving men a sense of freedom from impure wants and desires. James recognized the value and lasting benefits derived from one's own sorrow and suffering.

James led the church for nearly 30 years and is said to have played a key role in creating the Apostolic Decree (Acts 15) that ended the church's discriminatory practices against Gentiles converting to Christianity. Church elders insisted the Law of Moses dictated, among other things, that Gentiles must be circumcised if they desired to become Christians. James believed that giving their lives to Christ was sufficient and pushed to end the practice. From that point forward, Gentiles were asked only to abstain from sexual immorality and to avoid eating food sacrificed to idols or the meat of strangled animals.

James practiced what he preached. He was a strong advocate for prayer and believed that Christians should prove their faith through their actions and deeds. He was completely devoted to his prayer life. James's knees were said to have been compared to the knees of a camel because they were callused from spending long hours in prayer each day.

Historical accounts show that James died as a martyr in 62 A.D. He was reportedly taken to the top of the temple by the scribes and Pharisees and ordered to publicly denounce his Christian faith. Instead, James bravely professed his faith noting that Jesus was indeed the son of God and the Messiah. For this, James was thrown from the top of the temple to the ground. Because he survived the fall, he was then condemned to death by stoning.

Shortly before dying at the hands of his accusers, he repeated the same words uttered by Jesus at Calvary, "Father, forgive them for they know not what they do." James believed that Jesus gave His life for him, and in the end, James was willing to do the same for Jesus.

BOOK OF JAMES

NEW INTERNATIONAL VERSION (NIV)

1 James, a servant of God and of the Lord Jesus Christ,

To the twelve tribes scattered among the nations: Greetings.

TRIALS AND TEMPTATIONS

2 Consider it pure joy, my brothers and sisters, whenever you face trials of many kinds, **3** because you know that the testing of your faith produces perseverance. **4** Let perseverance finish its work so that you may be mature and complete, not lacking anything. **5** If any of you lacks wisdom, you should ask God, who gives generously to all without finding fault, and it will be given to you. **6** But when you ask, you must believe and not doubt, because the one who doubts is like a wave of the sea, blown and tossed by the wind. **7** That person should not expect to receive anything from the Lord. **8** Such a person is double-minded and unstable in all they do.

9 Believers in humble circumstances ought to take pride in their high position. **10** But the rich should take pride in their humiliation— since they will pass away like a wild flower. **11** For the sun rises with scorching heat and withers the plant; its blossom falls and its beauty is destroyed. In the same way, the rich will fade away even while they go about their business.

12 Blessed is the one who perseveres under trial because, having stood the test, that person will receive the crown of life that the Lord has promised to those who love him.

13 When tempted, no one should say, "God is tempting me." For God cannot be tempted by evil, nor does he tempt anyone; 14 but each person is tempted when they are dragged away by their own evil desire and enticed. 15 Then, after desire has conceived, it gives birth to sin; and sin, when it is full-grown, gives birth to death.

16 Don't be deceived, my dear brothers and sisters. 17 Every good and perfect gift is from above, coming down from the Father of the heavenly lights, who does not change like shifting shadows. 18 He chose to give us birth through the word of truth, that we might be a kind of firstfruits of all he created.

LISTENING AND DOING

19 My dear brothers and sisters, take note of this: Everyone should be quick to listen, slow to speak and slow to become angry, 20 because human anger does not produce the righteousness that God desires. 21 Therefore, get rid of all moral filth and the evil that is so prevalent and humbly accept the word planted in you, which can save you.

22 Do not merely listen to the word, and so deceive yourselves. Do what it says. 23 Anyone who listens to the word but does not do what it says is like someone who looks at his face in a mirror 24 and, after looking at himself, goes away and immediately forgets what he looks like. 25 But whoever looks intently into the perfect law that gives freedom, and continues in it—not forgetting what they have heard, but doing it—they will be blessed in what they do.

26 Those who consider themselves religious and yet do not keep a tight rein on their tongues deceive themselves, and their religion is worthless. 27 Religion that God our Father accepts as pure and

faultless is this: to look after orphans and widows in their distress and to keep oneself from being polluted by the world.

FAVORITISM FORBIDDEN

2 My brothers and sisters, believers in our glorious Lord Jesus Christ must not show favoritism. 2 Suppose a man comes into your meeting wearing a gold ring and fine clothes, and a poor man in filthy old clothes also comes in. 3 If you show special attention to the man wearing fine clothes and say, "Here's a good seat for you," but say to the poor man, "You stand there" or "Sit on the floor by my feet," 4 have you not discriminated among yourselves and become judges with evil thoughts?

5 Listen, my dear brothers and sisters: Has not God chosen those who are poor in the eyes of the world to be rich in faith and to inherit the kingdom he promised those who love him? 6 But you have dishonored the poor. Is it not the rich who are exploiting you? Are they not the ones who are dragging you into court? 7 Are they not the ones who are blaspheming the noble name of him to whom you belong?

8 If you really keep the royal law found in Scripture, "Love your neighbor as yourself," you are doing right. 9 But if you show favoritism, you sin and are convicted by the law as lawbreakers. 10 For whoever keeps the whole law and yet stumbles at just one point is guilty of breaking all of it. 11 For he who said, "You shall not commit adultery," also said, "You shall not murder." If you do not commit adultery but do commit murder, you have become a lawbreaker.

12 Speak and act as those who are going to be judged by the law that gives freedom, 13 because judgment without mercy will be shown to anyone who has not been merciful. Mercy triumphs over judgment.

FAITH AND DEEDS

14 What good is it, my brothers and sisters, if someone claims to have faith but has no deeds? Can such faith save them? **15** Suppose a brother or a sister is without clothes and daily food. **16** If one of you says to them, "Go in peace; keep warm and well fed," but does nothing about their physical needs, what good is it? **17** In the same way, faith by itself, if it is not accompanied by action, is dead.

18 But someone will say, "You have faith; I have deeds." Show me your faith without deeds, and I will show you my faith by my deeds. **19** You believe that there is one God. Good! Even the demons believe that—and shudder.

20 You foolish person, do you want evidence that faith without deeds is useless? **21** Was not our father Abraham considered righteous for what he did when he offered his son Isaac on the altar? **22** You see that his faith and his actions were working together, and his faith was made complete by what he did. **23** And the scripture was fulfilled that says, "Abraham believed God, and it was credited to him as righteousness," and he was called God's friend. **24** You see that a person is considered righteous by what they do and not by faith alone.

25 In the same way, was not even Rahab the prostitute considered righteous for what she did when she gave lodging to the spies and sent them off in a different direction? **26** As the body without the spirit is dead, so faith without deeds is dead.

TAMING THE TONGUE

3 Not many of you should become teachers, my fellow believers, because you know that we who teach will be judged more strictly.

2 We all stumble in many ways. Anyone who is never at fault in what they say is perfect, able to keep their whole body in check.

3 When we put bits into the mouths of horses to make them obey us, we can turn the whole animal. **4** Or take ships as an example. Although they are so large and are driven by strong winds, they are steered by a very small rudder wherever the pilot wants to go. **5** Likewise, the tongue is a small part of the body, but it makes great boasts. Consider what a great forest is set on fire by a small spark. **6** The tongue also is a fire, a world of evil among the parts of the body. It corrupts the whole body, sets the whole course of one's life on fire, and is itself set on fire by hell.

7 All kinds of animals, birds, reptiles and sea creatures are being tamed and have been tamed by mankind, **8** but no human being can tame the tongue. It is a restless evil, full of deadly poison.

9 With the tongue we praise our Lord and Father, and with it we curse human beings, who have been made in God's likeness. **10** Out of the same mouth come praise and cursing. My brothers and sisters, this should not be. **11** Can both fresh water and salt water flow from the same spring? **12** My brothers and sisters, can a fig tree bear olives, or a grapevine bear figs? Neither can a salt spring produce fresh water.

TWO KINDS OF WISDOM

13 Who is wise and understanding among you? Let them show it by their good life, by deeds done in the humility that comes from wisdom. **14** But if you harbor bitter envy and selfish ambition in your hearts, do not boast about it or deny the truth. **15** Such "wisdom" does not come down from heaven but is earthly, unspiritual, demonic. **16** For where you have envy and selfish ambition, there you find disorder and every evil practice.

17 But the wisdom that comes from heaven is first of all pure; then peace-loving, considerate, submissive, full of mercy and good fruit, impartial and sincere. **18** Peacemakers who sow in peace reap a harvest of righteousness.

SUBMIT YOURSELVES TO GOD

4 What causes fights and quarrels among you? Don't they come from your desires that battle within you? **2** You desire but do not have, so you kill. You covet but you cannot get what you want, so you quarrel and fight. You do not have because you do not ask God. **3** When you ask, you do not receive, because you ask with wrong motives, that you may spend what you get on your pleasures.

4 You adulterous people, don't you know that friendship with the world means enmity against God? Therefore, anyone who chooses to be a friend of the world becomes an enemy of God. **5** Or do you think Scripture says without reason that he jealously longs for the spirit he has caused to dwell in us? **6** But he gives us more grace. That is why Scripture says:

> "God opposes the proud
> but shows favor to the humble."

7 Submit yourselves, then, to God. Resist the devil, and he will flee from you. **8** Come near to God and he will come near to you. Wash your hands, you sinners, and purify your hearts, you double-minded. **9** Grieve, mourn and wail. Change your laughter to mourning and your joy to gloom. **10** Humble yourselves before the Lord, and he will lift you up.

11 Brothers and sisters, do not slander one another. Anyone who speaks against a brother or sister or judges them speaks against the law and judges it. When you judge the law, you are not keeping it, but sitting in judgment on it. 12 There is only one Lawgiver and Judge, the one who is able to save and destroy. But you—who are you to judge your neighbor?

BOASTING ABOUT TOMORROW

13 Now listen, you who say, "Today or tomorrow we will go to this or that city, spend a year there, carry on business and make money." 14 Why, you do not even know what will happen tomorrow. What is your life? You are a mist that appears for a little while and then vanishes. 15 Instead, you ought to say, "If it is the Lord's will, we will live and do this or that." 16 As it is, you boast in your arrogant schemes. All such boasting is evil. 17 If anyone, then, knows the good they ought to do and doesn't do it, it is sin for them.

WARNING TO RICH OPPRESSORS

5 Now listen, you rich people, weep and wail because of the misery that is coming on you. 2 Your wealth has rotted, and moths have eaten your clothes. 3 Your gold and silver are corroded. Their corrosion will testify against you and eat your flesh like fire. You have hoarded wealth in the last days. 4 Look! The wages you failed to pay the workers who mowed your fields are crying out against you. The cries of the harvesters have reached the ears of the Lord Almighty. 5 You have lived on earth in luxury and self-indulgence. You have fattened yourselves in the day of slaughter. 6 You have condemned and murdered the innocent one, who was not opposing you.

PATIENCE IN SUFFERING

7 Be patient, then, brothers and sisters, until the Lord's coming. See how the farmer waits for the land to yield its valuable crop, patiently waiting for the autumn and spring rains. 8 You too, be patient and stand firm, because the Lord's coming is near. 9 Don't grumble against one another, brothers and sisters, or you will be judged. The Judge is standing at the door!

10 Brothers and sisters, as an example of patience in the face of suffering, take the prophets who spoke in the name of the Lord. 11 As you know, we count as blessed those who have persevered. You have heard of Job's perseverance and have seen what the Lord finally brought about. The Lord is full of compassion and mercy.

12 Above all, my brothers and sisters, do not swear—not by heaven or by earth or by anything else. All you need to say is a simple "Yes" or "No." Otherwise you will be condemned.

THE PRAYER OF FAITH

13 Is anyone among you in trouble? Let them pray. Is anyone happy? Let them sing songs of praise. 14 Is anyone among you sick? Let them call the elders of the church to pray over them and anoint them with oil in the name of the Lord. 15 And the prayer offered in faith will make the sick person well; the Lord will raise them up. If they have sinned, they will be forgiven. 16 Therefore confess your sins to each other and pray for each other so that you may be healed. The prayer of a righteous person is powerful and effective.

17 Elijah was a human being, even as we are. He prayed earnestly that it would not rain, and it did not rain on the land for three and a half

years. **18** Again he prayed, and the heavens gave rain, and the earth produced its crops.

19 My brothers and sisters, if one of you should wander from the truth and someone should bring tthat person back, **20** remember this: Whoever turns a sinner from the error of their way will save them from death and cover over a multitude of sins.

INSPIRATION

THE MAN IN THE ARENA

"It is not the critic who counts; not the man who points out how the strong man stumbles, or where the doer of deeds could have done them better. The credit belongs to the man who is actually in the arena, whose face is marred by dust and sweat and blood; who strives valiantly; who errs, who comes short again and again, because there is no effort without error and shortcoming; but who does actually strive to do the deeds; who knows great enthusiasms, the great devotions; who spends himself in a worthy cause; who at the best knows in the end the triumph of high achievement, and who at the worst, if he fails, at least fails while daring greatly, so that his place shall never be with those cold and timid souls who neither know victory nor defeat."

— Teddy Roosevelt
Excerpt from the speech "Citizenship In A Republic"
delivered at the Sorbonne, in Paris, France on April 23, 1910

EMBRACE YOUR STRUGGLES

Consider it pure joy, my brothers and sisters, whenever you face trials of many kinds, because you know that the testing of your faith produces perseverance. Let perseverance finish its work so that you may be mature and complete, not lacking anything. (James 1:2-4 NIV)

For most of us, the natural reaction to an unexpected challenge or setback is to become angry and disappointed. When life starts heading down a path we didn't anticipate; our masculine instinct is to power up in an effort to mask the fear that sets in when we don't have absolute control over a given situation.

If we instead looked at these trials as mere speed bumps on the road of life, we would slow down and see that God has a great purpose in each of these challenges.

For those of us who have lived through a cancer diagnosis, a child's addiction issues, or the sudden loss of a loved one, we know these setbacks initially seem devastating. In retrospect, though, we can recognize that the experience brought us wisdom and a new perspective on life. In many cases, our faith becomes stronger when it is tested because we discover God's constant presence and learn that He will never give us more than we can handle.

In Romans 5:3, Paul tells us to find joy in our tribulations. We should embrace the tough times as much as we savor the good moments in life. Think of your faith like a muscle; the more you exercise your faith, the stronger it becomes.

Through good times and bad, God has an amazing plan for our lives. All we have to do is surrender ourselves to His will and trust Him to lead us through the trials that initially appear to be insurmountable.

MY PRAYER

God, give me the courage to surrender to Your will and place my complete trust in Your divine plan for my life. Amen.

READ	2 CORINTHIANS 4:7-11

RESPOND

- *What are the most significant challenges you've faced in your life?*
- *Looking back on those challenges, what did you learn about God's nature through those experiences?*

CONTEMPLATE

- *Recall a time when you encountered a challenge that seemed overwhelming. Share the details about the state of your emotions and how that challenge was eventually resolved.*

PRAY FOR WISDOM

If any of you lacks wisdom, you should ask God, who gives generously to all without finding fault, and it will be given to you. (James 1:5 NIV)

There's an almost supernatural phenomenon that occurs when we seek wisdom from God. It doesn't matter what your circumstances might be, or where you are in your spiritual journey. God imparts distinct wisdom in our hearts and minds when we seek Him.

It's hard to describe the sensation other than to say that it's as if the Holy Spirit gives us access to a universe of understanding that did not exist before. If you're a skeptic, you're likely to have serious doubts about this concept until you experience it for yourself.

Proverbs 3:13 says, "Happy is the man who finds wisdom and the man who gets understanding." God's willingness to give us wisdom begins with our own earnest desire to know Him as well as we can. Part of this process begins by spending time in the Word, reading of the testimonies and laws that God has put forth.

We must then pray for discernment with a pure heart and a commitment to deepen our faith. We must then go to Jesus with a plan to put our faith in action. We must meet God where He is and accept his mercy, dedicating our hearts to knowing and loving Him more than anything else we've ever loved.

We should not pray for God to solve our problems but rather for Him to see us through our challenges by imparting His divine wisdom. Our heartfelt desire should be to use this newfound wisdom for the purpose of glorifying God through our service and love for our neighbors. God will bestow upon us a unique understanding so that we can overcome our challenges as we endeavor to strengthen our relationships, solidify our families and live exemplary lives.

MY PRAYER

God, open my heart and mind to receive Your divine wisdom so that I can make a difference in my life and in the world You created. Let me use this gift of wisdom to better serve others and lead a life that is worthy of the gift You have given me. Amen.

READ	PROVERBS 4:10-27

RESPOND

- *God meets us where we are, regardless of where we are in our journey. In what area of your life could you benefit most from God's wisdom?*

- *Can you recall a time in your life when asking God for wisdom might have changed the outcome of a given situation? Describe.*

CONTEMPLATE

- *What do you know about God that gives you the confidence to believe He will give you the wisdom you need?*

STOP WORRYING

If any of you lacks wisdom, you should ask God, who gives generously to all without finding fault, and it will be given to you. But when you ask, you must believe and not doubt, because the one who doubts is like a wave of the sea, blown and tossed by the wind. (James 1:5-6 NIV)

We spend so much of our time worrying about things over which we have little control. Whether we're worrying about personal finances, health concerns or a loved one's bad choices, we can't change the outcome by stewing about it. In fact, constant worry can be destructive and take its toll on our health and our relationships.

God wants us to find peace by placing our burdens on Him. Instead of being worriers, we must become warriors.

In Matthew 11:28-30, we are told that Jesus offers rest and peace to the weary and burdened. Worrying should not be a habit for those who have a strong faith or those who trust completely in God.

Many of us live by the myth that if we want something done right, we must do it ourselves. No matter how much we desire to have total control over our lives, we don't have the resourcefulness of our loving God, nor do we have the wisdom to know what's ultimately best for our lives.

When we allow God to give wisdom to our problems, we gain a new perspective once our burdens are lifted. We can trust that God will shed new light on our problems and He will deliver us from worry. God may not solve our problems in the way we desire, but we can take comfort in knowing that He is definitely with us in our problems.

Wisdom has been defined as "dynamic insight into the ways and purpose of God." God doesn't take us out of every problem. More often than not, He takes us through our problems. From this develops our ability to believe and see how God is using our difficulties for our good and the good of others.

MY PRAYER

God, help me to surrender my life to You so that I can be free from worry. You are my comfort and my strength. I place my trust in You. Amen.

READ	MATTHEW 6:25-34

RESPOND

- *How prevalent is worry in your life?*

- *What do you know about God's characteristics that gives you the confidence that He can take away your worry?*

CONTEMPLATE

- *Write a prayer to God that addresses the one concern about which you worry most.*

PRACTICE HUMILITY

Believers in humble circumstances ought to take pride in their high position. But the rich should take pride in their humiliation — since they will pass away like a wild flower. (James 1:9-10 NIV)

We are competitive creatures by nature. We keep score in nearly every aspect of our lives. We tend to be obsessed with the number of things we own as compared to our neighbors, friends, and relatives.

Somewhere along the way, we learned that our self-worth is somehow connected to our worldly possessions, the rank we've achieved, or the number of trophies on the bookshelf. In spite of these obsessions, we strive to gain favor with a God who doesn't keep score, a God who loves us unconditionally regardless of our position in life.

The truth is that God looks with favor on the least among us, a notion that seems to contrast wildly with the norms and practices of today's "Me Generation." For men, our pride is our most destructive sin. We live in a society where we've been told that we have to be smarter, quicker and hungrier for success than the guy sitting next to us.

We let our fear, pride, anxiety, and shame separate us from God. We should feel humbled by our position in life knowing that 100 percent of our blessings have come from our generous and loving God.

Psalm 149:4 tells us that God crowns the humble among us with the gift of salvation. Every one of us falls short of God's glory, and none of us deserve the place that's been set aside for us in heaven. We would be wise to set aside our arrogant ways and focus on living gratefully for the grace and mercy extended to us in Christ (Ephesians 2:8-9).

MY PRAYER

God, help me to set aside my boastful ways. Empower me to follow and embrace the example of humility set forth by Your son, our savior Jesus Christ. Amen.

READ	JOHN 13:1-16

RESPOND

- *What are some of the ways in which you "keep score" with those around you?*

- *In what area of your life does the act of humility come most naturally? How can you use this experience to practice humility in the areas of your life where it is a struggle?*

CONTEMPLATE

- *Compile a list of the blessings in your life for which you are most grateful.*

BE PERSISTENT

Blessed is the one who perseveres under trial because, having stood the test, that person will receive the crown of life that the Lord has promised to those who love him. (James 1:12 NIV)

Life can be overwhelming at times. The pressure we put on ourselves to juggle the demands of a career with the responsibilities of being a father and husband can cause us to retreat to harmful vices or to abandon our loved ones. The added pressure of living the picture-perfect life is enough to make us feel like throwing in the towel.

Our egos tell us we would rather quit than fail. However, for those who persevere, God offers a great reward that makes the struggle seem like a relatively small sacrifice.

If you've ever known someone who has run a marathon, you probably know that accomplishing that feat takes months of preparation. Through rain or shine, snow and heat, the runner must push through long runs and withstand the physical toll it takes on his body. Even for those who forge ahead in their preparation, the day of the race is still fraught with challenges.

Marathon runners often describe the sensation of "hitting the wall" in the final leg of the race where it seems nearly impossible to keep running. As with life, those who persevere will receive a great reward. Beyond earning a medal, the immense satisfaction of crossing that finish line is unlike any other feeling.

Steadfast is the man who is not distracted from his mission when facing life's greatest challenges. In Matthew 5:11-12, Jesus describes a reward in heaven that diminishes the pain and sacrifice we've endured in our pursuit to finish the race.

Throughout life, there is usually a direct correlation between the effort you expend and the reward you reap. In an era when immediate gratification is in such high demand, be reminded that a slow and steady pursuit of the finish line still wins the race.

MY PRAYER
God, let me be steadfast in pursuing that which awaits me in Your Kingdom. Give me the stamina and determination to persevere through this life's greatest challenges so that I may live in eternity in Your presence.

READ	LUKE 11:5-9

RESPOND
- *In what ways do you want God to reward you for your perseverance?*

- *In what areas of your life would you benefit from being more persistent?*

CONTEMPLATE
- *What do you believe about God's nature that will help you overcome any challenge you face in the future?*

OVERCOME TEMPTATION

When tempted, no one should say, "God is tempting me." For God cannot be tempted by evil, nor does he tempt anyone; but each person is tempted when they are dragged away by their own evil desire and enticed. (James 1:13-14)

Are you familiar with the seven deadly sins? They are gluttony, envy, sloth, wrath, pride, lust and greed. These sins have amazing power over our lives. No matter how much willpower and discipline we muster in our efforts to resist them, we too often give in to the temptation.

To make matters worse, Satan plays a cruel game of spiritual warfare with these sins and is constantly looking for opportunities to prey on our weakness. Unfortunately, we are easy targets. Through his mercy and grace, God gives us the tools we need to stand firm and avoid temptation. The best news is that even when we fail, God offers us forgiveness.

God does not create temptation because He only wants what's best for us. However, He still gives us the free will to make our own decisions, and this is where we wrestle with the temptation that is driven by our sinful desires.

While we may believe that many of our sins are victimless, there's a cascading effect when we give in to temptation and let ourselves be enticed by sin. It's a slippery slope that can be avoided only if we put our moral values on a solid foundation. When we succumb to the enticements of pornography, alcohol abuse and fits of anger, we create fertile ground for Satan.

God can protect us from the temptations that are more than we can bear. He also gives us the gift of discernment to help us avoid behaviors that will derail us. While God gives us a way to escape from sin, we must decide for ourselves to be obedient. The desire to sin doesn't go away, but our ability to resist temptation will increase the more we lean into God and place our trust in Him.

MY PRAYER
God, give me the wisdom and discernment to know when I am setting myself up for failure. Give me an earnest desire to resist sin and temptation in my daily life. Teach me to be obedient in all that I do. Amen.

READ	**MATTHEW 4:1-11**

RESPOND
- *Which of the seven deadly sins do you struggle with most?*

- *Under what circumstances or conditions do you feel most vulnerable to sin?*

CONTEMPLATE
- *Based on your understanding of God's relationship with mankind, why did He give us the free will to make decisions that might be harmful to us?*

PRACTICE PATIENCE

My dear brothers and sisters, take note of this: Everyone should be quick to listen, slow to speak and slow to become angry because human anger does not produce the righteousness that God desires. (James 1:19-20 NIV)

Patience is indeed a virtue. Perhaps you've heard the phrase "the patience of Job," which comes from the Old Testament lesson of a faithful servant of God named Job, who lost all of his children and his wealth in one day. On top of that, he developed painful sores all over his body and received no empathy from his wife or his friends. Despite his many setbacks, Job remained faithful to God even when he didn't know what God was doing. He remained patient.

The trials we face today pale in comparison to Job's predicament, giving us affirmation that we, like Job, can grow by patiently trusting God.

Being patient requires a strong sense of self-awareness about our feelings and insecurities. When men perceive threats to their masculinity and dominance, we often lose patience with those around us because we feel as if we're losing control over some aspect of our lives. We like to be in control of our circumstances at all times.

Unfortunately, we too often fail to accurately assess situations. Rather than putting our trust in God and giving Him control in the most challenging moments of our lives, we feel compelled to dig in and defend our positions, with or without the facts.

Proverbs 3:5-6 tells us to put our trust in God and do not rely on our own understanding of the facts. By submitting to God, we give Him the opportunity to give us the wisdom to make things right. The next time you feel a situation spinning out of control, take a deep breath and turn to God for clarity and understanding. You'll find the peace you're looking for if you pause, reflect and then respond.

MY PRAYER
God, give me the patience of Job. Open my heart, my mind, and my ears so that I can have the peace and understanding you desire for me. Amen.

READ	HEBREWS 10:35-38

RESPOND
- *Describe the situations that typically cause you to lose patience with those around you.*

- *What are the areas of your life in which you feel you could exert a stronger sense of emotional self-control for the benefit of all involved?*

CONTEMPLATE
- *Reflect on a time in your life when you lost patience with someone close to you. What were the causes? What was the result?*

MIND YOUR TEMPER

My dear brothers and sisters, take note of this: Everyone should be quick to listen, slow to speak and slow to become angry because human anger does not produce the righteousness that God desires. (James 1:19-20 NIV)

Men often get mixed messages about expressing their emotions. Some men let their emotions bottle up because they've been taught to suppress their feelings. Others were encouraged to express their anger, to get things off our chest and not hold back! Ultimately, the manner in which we respond is often the difference between sinful and acceptable behavior. While there may be a time and place for every type of emotional response, scripture tells us that giving in to our temper is a sin.

It's usually the quick bursts of temper that get us in the most trouble. Proverbs 14:17 says that a man with a quick temper is a fool, while Proverbs 15:1 tells us that the man who maintains a calm, even temper is easier to live with.

God wants us to live in accordance with the nine attributes of the Fruit of the Holy Spirit. They are love, joy, peace, patience, kindness, goodness, faithfulness, gentleness and self-control. While these don't sound like the cornerstones of a masculine life, learning to live in this manner will improve even our most complicated relationships.

Instead of reacting in anger, God wants us to respond with forgiveness and not seek vengeance for the offenses against us. That's a tough pill to swallow, but it gives us the opportunity to check our motivations while we contemplate the appropriate response.

Anger can be a valid emotion, and it isn't always sinful, but a hasty response rarely yields the results we are seeking. Slowing things down a bit so that we can gain wisdom and focus is a true sign of one's strong faith.

MY PRAYER

God, let me be slow to anger. Grant me the patience and humility I need to contemplate the effect of my response to those who offend or harm me. Let my response be a righteous glorification of You. Amen.

READ	PETER 1:5-9

RESPOND

- *Which of the nine attributes of a Fruitful Spirit is the easiest for you to embrace? Why?*

- *Which of the nine attributes of a Fruitful Spirit is the most difficult for you to embrace? Why?*

CONTEMPLATE

- *Based on your understanding of God's nature, explain why losing your temper is considered a sin.*

ACT ON YOUR FAITH

Do not merely listen to the word, and so deceive yourselves.
Do what it says. (James 1:22-23 NIV)

What you do is often much more important than what you say.
It's one thing to grow your faith by reading the Bible, praying or
memorizing scripture, but if you don't initiate the kind of actions
that match the premise of your faith, you really aren't living up to the
standards that make you a strong Christian.

We will learn later that faith without deeds is worthless, but the
bottom line is that your actions must match your words. You can say
you love your neighbor, but if you're not willing to feed them when
they're hungry or offer shelter when they are homeless, your faith
lacks authenticity.

There are countless opportunities to put your faith into action. Whether
you're willing to work in a soup kitchen, volunteer at a homeless
shelter, or simply rake leaves for an elderly person, you can show your
unconditional love for others through simple acts of kindness.

Many churches work hard to attract newcomers to their Sunday
services but fail to realize that taking their faith outside the church
walls would be more effective in showing others the good that
Christians can do.

You can attend church every Sunday and read your Bible every morning, but if you don't put some action behind your faith, you're experiencing only a small portion of what it's really like to lead a Christ-centered life. The best way to show someone that you're a Christian is to let your actions speak for themselves. You might be surprised by how much you can teach people about the love of Christ without saying a single word.

MY PRAYER

God, help me demonstrate my Christian faith by serving others so that they will know You through my acts of kindness, even when my words fall short. May You be glorified in all that I do in serving others. Amen.

READ	LUKE 10:25-37

RESPOND

- *In what ways do your actions align with, or fall short of, your spoken faith?*

- *How might serving others help you in your own spiritual journey?*

CONTEMPLATE

- *Write a prayer asking God to guide you in your endeavors to serve others.*

TAME THE TONGUE

Those who consider themselves religious and yet do not keep a tight rein on their tongues deceive themselves, and their religion is worthless. (James 1:26 NIV)

It's been said that man's words reveal the condition of his heart. The words we use are a reflection of our character. Unfortunately, human nature dictates that the more we talk, the more likely we are to sin. It's as if we run out of things to say once we get beyond the customary discussion of news, weather, and sports. From that point, our conversations typically devolve into the latest gossip and our chatter is usually peppered with cursing and foul language. God wants us to bring things up a notch.

Proverbs 17:28 tells us that even the most foolish among us seem wise when they are silent. Those are great words of advice. Because of our various stages of woundedness, so many of us unconsciously use words as a defense mechanism to keep others at a safe distance.

We fail to recognize the true impact of these words on the people who desire to be closer to us. In instances like these, our words are poisonous, even when our intentions are exactly the opposite.

God wants our words to reflect the love and respect we have in our hearts for Him when we are talking to others. If our faith is weak or shallow, people will know it immediately by the words we use.

You've heard the old saying, "If you can't say something nice, don't say anything at all!" In most cases, it's as simple as taking the time to think before we speak. Doing so gives you a better chance of showing God's love in the way we connect with others.

MY PRAYER

God, give me discernment when I speak so that my words will glorify You and the works You have done through the universe. Let my words and actions demonstrate my faithfulness to You. Amen.

READ	MATTHEW 15:10-20

RESPOND

- *When are you most likely to gossip or curse in conversations with others?*

- *Do you believe that your language accurately reflects what's in your heart? Why or why not?*

CONTEMPLATE

- *How can you use your words to serve God and build bridges with others?*

BE COMPASSIONATE

Listen, my dear brothers and sisters: Has not God chosen those who are poor in the eyes of the world to be rich in faith and to inherit the kingdom he promised those who love him? (James 2:5 NIV)

None of us have control over the circumstances into which we are born. Some of us were lucky enough to have both a mother and father in the home, while others drew an even better straw and were born into homes where there were few concerns regarding food, shelter or safety. Even those born into less fortunate circumstances including poverty or nontraditional families realize their good fortune compared to those living in third world countries where disease, malnutrition, and violence are part of everyday life.

No matter the lot we've been assigned in life, it's clear that our situation has always been dependent on the grace and mercy of a loving God.

The Bible is full of teachings regarding how we should take care of those who are hungry, thirsty, impoverished, sick and imprisoned. Matthew 25:31-46 tells us that God wants us to know that we can expect to be treated in the same manner in which we have treated the least among us.

It's only by God's grace that we are not living under what would seem like impossible conditions. We, therefore, have a duty and responsibility to share our good fortune by taking care of those who need our help.

When we serve those less fortunate, we serve and honor God. Showing any form of apathy or lack of interest in these circumstances is actually a sign of weak faith, demonstrating we have not been transformed by the grace of Jesus Christ. There is an eternal reward for our kindness to those in need. We serve God by serving others.

MY PRAYER
God, give me a heart that instinctively serves others, especially those less fortunate. Help me seek out opportunities to help others and let me do so with a servant's heart. Amen.

READ	DEUTERONOMY 15:7-11

RESPOND
- *Why do you believe we are obligated to take care of those in need?*

- *In addition to the hungry, thirsty, impoverished, sick, and imprisoned, what other groups of people would benefit from your support?*

CONTEMPLATE
- *If you were among the needy in your community, how would you hope to be treated by those who have been blessed?*

AVOID FAVORITISM

My brothers and sisters, believers in our glorious Lord Jesus Christ must not show favoritism. Suppose a man comes into your meeting wearing a gold ring and fine clothes, and a poor man in filthy old clothes also comes in. If you show special attention to the man wearing fine clothes and say, "Here's a good seat for you," but say to the poor man, "You stand there," or "Sit on the floor by my feet," have you not discriminated among yourselves and become judges with evil thoughts? (James 2:1-4 NIV)

All of us were made in God's image. Our ethnicity, race, gender or social status make no difference to God. We are all the same: perfectly created and loved equally in His eyes. God sees us as equals, and that's exactly the way He wants us to see others. More than just loving our neighbors, God wants us to love everyone on this earth regardless of how or where we encounter them.

In his life here on earth, Jesus made it known that the Ten Commandments were embodied in loving God and loving others. This is the Great Commandment, not just one or the other, but both.

How would we treat Jesus if he were to return to the earth looking as he did when he lived here? After all, Jesus led a fairly nomadic life and was known to associate with tax collectors, lepers, prostitutes and some of society's most rejected people. Would we recognize Jesus? Would we be able to distinguish Him from a person that we believed to be homeless?

As much as you love Jesus, would you pass over him as someone we deemed as a societal reject? One way to avoid this possibility is to start looking for Jesus in every person we encounter.

Loving a stranger may seem far outside of our comfort zones, but that's what God has called us to do. If Christ has accepted this person and gave His life for their sins, shouldn't we be willing to bring that same person into our hearts? Isn't that what God has done for us? In the end, God is the ultimate judge. We will be unworthy of His mercy if we can't love those who have been made in His image.

MY PRAYER

God, let me love others in the authentic way You have shown in Your love for me. Release me from my inhibitions and discomfort so that I may extend the unconditional love that is mine to give. Amen.

READ	1 JOHN 4:7-12

RESPOND

- *What are the risks associated with showing compassion to a complete stranger?*

- *What are the possible benefits associated with showing compassion to a complete stranger?*

CONTEMPLATE

- *Write about what God is calling you to do in regard to showing compassion for the least among us.*

LIVE CONSISTENTLY

For whoever keeps the whole law and yet stumbles at just one point is guilty of breaking all of it. (James 2:10 NIV)

You might be one of those guys who would never, under any circumstance, tell a lie. Your friends say that you're as honest as the day is long. You might even be one of those guys who has a miniature version of the Ten Commandments tablets tattooed on your left forearm, and you pride yourself on being true to God's law 99.9% of the time.

Your only weakness may be that you have a wandering eye. Sometimes, when nobody is looking, you sneak a peek at pornography or give a lustful stare when an attractive woman walks by. Beyond that, you're an all around good Christian, right? Wrong. In God's eyes, having a lustful thought is the equivalent of committing adultery. Sin, no matter the degree, is still sin. God hates sin.

In Romans 3:23, we are reminded that all people sin and we all fall short of the glory of God. Even though we know of God's disdain for sin, some of us will still accept His remarkable gift of grace and forgiveness and just keep sinning.

We lose sight of the fact that the Ten Commandments were not brought down from the mountaintop and presented to us as a multiple choice test or as a moral smorgasbord. We can't selectively pick and choose which of God's laws we want to embrace and those we want to ignore. If we break any part of God's law, we've broken all of God's law. Like a chain, if we've broken one link, we've broken the whole chain.

God knows what is in our hearts. Regardless of our intentions, we are called to be righteous in all that we do. It's not possible to be a part-time follower of Christ because God wants 100 percent of us. When the day comes that we find ourselves in the arms of Jesus Christ, we want every part of our body and soul to be pure. Living a life that is free of sin may seem like a tall order, but it's nonetheless what we should strive to be every day of our lives.

MY PRAYER
God, give me the discipline and desire to follow all Your laws. Keep me ever mindful of Your commandments and guide me toward freeing my life from the sin that separates me from You. Amen.

READ	1 JOHN 2:3-11

RESPOND

- *In what areas of your life do you most often fall short of living a life that pleases God?*

- *When you consider the areas of your life where you most consistently fall short of God's glory, identify the 'triggers' that tend to lead you down this path.*

CONTEMPLATE

- *Write about the areas of your life that you believe to be pleasing to God.*

BE MERCIFUL

Speak and act as those who are going to be judged by the law that gives freedom, because judgment without mercy will be shown to anyone who has not been merciful. Mercy triumphs over judgment. (James 2:12-13 NIV)

If you are a follower of Christ, you probably have experienced the wonder of God's mercy. For mere mortals, the most common way to extend mercy is by offering forgiveness to those who have wronged us in some way.

Many of us struggle with the idea of clearing the slate with someone who has cheated us, caused harm or injury, or treated us unfairly. We often forget that God's mercy has been extended to us because he gave His only son to die in exchange for our sins.

To put the concept of mercy in its proper context, it's important to know that justice is essentially getting what we deserve. For example, if we have treated someone unfairly, justice comes when we are punished for our actions.

Mercy is when God chooses not to punish us even though we deserve it. Grace is when we receive blessings from God when we don't deserve them. The mercy and grace that God extends to us are amazing gifts.

Jesus uses the parable of the unmerciful servant (Matthew 18: 21-35) to remind us that we should, in like manner, extend mercy to others. No matter how egregious the sin or infraction against us, we should offer forgiveness, unconditionally. When we fail to extend mercy, we show the world the weakness of our faith. We honor God when we extend these gifts to others, especially when they may not deserve it.

MY PRAYER

God, teach me to forgive my debtors in the way that my debts have been forgiven. Make me ever mindful of the sacrifice You made so that I might have the opportunity to live in eternity with You. Amen.

READ	MATTHEW 18: 21-35

RESPOND

- *Can you recall a time in your life when someone extended mercy to you? How did that make you feel?*

- *Is there someone to whom you have failed to extend mercy?*

CONTEMPLATE

- *How has your life been affected by God's grace and mercy?*

AVOID HYPOCRISY

What good is it, my brothers, if someone says he has faith but does not have works? Can that faith save him? If a brother or sister is poorly clothed and lacking in daily food, and one of you says to them, "Go in peace, be warmed and filled," without giving them the things needed for the body, what good is that? So also faith by itself, if it does not have works, is dead. But someone will say, "You have faith and I have works." Show me your faith apart from your works, and I will show you my faith by my works. (James 2:14-26 NIV)

Hypocrisy can best be defined as the disparity that exists between the image we try to project and the reality of our actual character. The root word hypo is derived from the Greek word for "actor." A hypocrite is someone who pretends to be something they aren't.

A hypocrite's words and works do not align with his faith. You can sit in the front row of church every Sunday, but if you go home and verbally or emotionally abuse your family, you're a hypocrite.

If you've spent much time studying scripture, you might be familiar with the conflict that existed between Jesus and the Pharisees. This group of exalted religious leaders was well versed in Scripture and God's laws, but they had no compassion for their fellow man.

Jesus called them out for their lack of mercy and unwillingness to help those in need. Jesus referred to these types of Christians as "wolves in sheep's clothing" (Matthew 7:15) and whitewashed tombs (Matthew 23:27).

If we desire to live a Christ-centered life, we must maintain consistency between what we believe in our hearts and how we live our lives. We should never be concerned with justifying ourselves before men, but instead seeking God with a heart full of compassion for the least among us and for those who will see God glorified by our actions.

MY PRAYER

God, let my actions match what's in my heart. Let me live a life that is not only consistent with your laws but also filled with an abundance of love for others. Amen.

READ	MATTHEW 7:1-5

RESPOND

- *How does your life as a Christian align with your professional life? Are you the same person at work as you are at church?*

- *How does your life at home align with your professional life? Are you the same person at home as you are at work?*

CONTEMPLATE

- *Write about the disparities that currently exist in your life. What are the differences between the person you are and the person you want to be?*

AVOID COMPLACENCY

You foolish person, do you want evidence that faith without deeds is useless? Was not our father Abraham considered righteous for what he did when he offered his son Isaac on the altar? You see that his faith and his actions were working together, and his faith was made complete by what he did. (James 2:20-22 NIV)

As men, we tend to gravitate toward systems and patterns that are familiar to us. The older we get, the more dedicated we become to our morning routines, schedules, and traditions. We like consistency and normalcy, and heaven help the person who tries to interrupt our established patterns of behavior.

As Christians, we need to mix things up. We cannot let our desire for contentment and comfort make us complacent. There will be times when God wants to stretch us and move us toward greater challenges so we can deepen our faith.

For men, few things are as comforting as the status quo, but there are times when we need to be shoved out of our comfort zones. When you think about it, a big part of our church life is filled with complacency. We go to the same service every weekend, and we sit in the exact same spot every week. God wants us to step up and branch out, meet new people, try new things, and reach outside our respective centers of influence to touch new lives.

For example, in Matthew 28:16-20, you'll find what is commonly referred to as The Great Commission where Jesus calls his followers to go out and spread the good news of the gospel.

Jesus wants all of us to become His disciples and to become fishers of men. If we're too comfortable with where we are, we'll miss an amazing opportunity to give new life to our Christian journey.

MY PRAYER

God, give me the energy and desire to constantly find new ways to put my faith in action and to spread the word of Your good news. Allow me to be content without becoming complacent in the ways that I can serve You. Amen.

READ	1 TIMOTHY 6: 6-12

RESPOND

- *In what area of your life are you most complacent?*

- *What would you say is the difference between contentment and complacency?*

CONTEMPLATE

- *Write about a time in your life when you were pushed outside of your comfort zone. Why was it uncomfortable? What was the outcome?*

WATCH YOUR WORDS

Or take ships as an example. Although they are so large and are driven by strong winds, they are steered by a very small rudder wherever the pilot wants to go. Likewise, the tongue is a small part of the body, but it makes great boasts. Consider what a great forest is set on fire by a small spark. The tongue also is a fire, a world of evil among the parts of the body. It corrupts the whole body, sets the whole course of one's life on fire, and is itself set on fire by hell. (James 3:4-6 NIV)

Perhaps you remember this saying from childhood: "Sticks and stones will break my bones, but words will never hurt me." At the time we were reciting this phrase, we were telling those who were taunting us that their cruel words didn't sting. As it turns out, nothing could have been further from the truth.

The messages we received as children were seared into our subconscious state, only to return years later to mess with our self-esteem. It was one thing to hear harmful words from other children, but something far more damaging to hear those words from a parent, teacher or coach. God wants us to be mindful of the power of our words and how they profoundly affect others

The analogy comparing a ship's rudder to the tongue is powerful. In Ephesians 4:29, we are taught that the only words that should come out of our mouths are those that build up and extend grace to others. Imagine if everyone lived by that wisdom?

Rather than spending large chunks of our lives trying to reconcile someone's off-handed remarks with our true identity, we could focus our energies on building lives that are happy, content and meaningful.

Our challenge is to heed this advice in our daily contact with others, but especially with our children and other loved ones. Imagine how words of encouragement, rather than criticism, might have changed the course of your own life. We have a unique opportunity to serve God by using our words to build up rather than tear down.

MY PRAYER

God, let my words build up, rather than destroy. Let the words from my mouth and the meditations of my heart be pleasing and acceptable in Your sight, O God, my Rock, and my Redeemer. Amen.

READ   **1 THESSALONIANS 5:11-22**

RESPOND

- *How has someone's criticism of you when you were young affected you later in life?*

- *How did someone's words of encouragement or praise affect you?*

CONTEMPLATE

- *Write about an experience from your youth when you were criticized or affirmed by someone else's words. What was the lasting impact?*

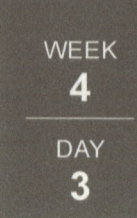

CURB AMBITION

For where you have envy and selfish ambition, there you find disorder and every evil practice. (James 3:16 NIV)

Envy. Pride. Ambition. Ever since the origin of sin in the Garden of Eden, these are the traits that have prevented us from achieving exemplary lives of contentment and happiness. Our desire to have the things that belong to other people have driven us to sin. We are envious of other men's homes, cars, jobs and, yes, even their wives. It is a sin to covet what others have. God wants us to be content with what we've been given.

In Luke 12:15 we are reminded that worldly possessions don't define us or the way that God looks at us. Nor do our belongings determine how others should view us. We will ultimately be judged by our actions, specifically in the way we treat others.

Unfortunately, we instinctively get it wrong all the time. Our desire to achieve significance through wealth prevents us from finding contentment in our lives. Ambition can be a positive component of our lives, but only when we use it for the benefit of serving others and God.

As we mature, our perspective begins to change. You've heard the saying, "You can't take it with you." It rings true when you realize that the treasures of this earth are worthless in God's kingdom and may be a wedge that separates us from Him. When we take an inventory of our non-material blessings, we begin to recognize what's truly important. Once we become satisfied with what God has given us, joy will return to our lives in immeasurable ways.

MY PRAYER

God, teach me to be grateful for all that I have in my life. Guide me in redirecting my ambition for the good of others and for finding ways to serve You. Amen.

READ	MATTHEW 6:19-21

RESPOND

- *In what part of your life do you struggle most with envy?*

- *In what part of your life do you struggle most with pride?*

CONTEMPLATE

- *In what areas of your life do you feel the greatest sense of contentment? Why?*

SOW PEACE

Peacemakers who sow in peace reap a harvest of righteousness.
(James 3:18 NIV)

The world seems to be full of conflict and chaos. As a result, it's easy for us to find a high degree of dissatisfaction in so many areas of our lives. The tension that comes when we're unhappy with our careers, personal relationships, or even our spiritual journey can be destructive. Our inability to derive a sense of satisfaction in these areas demonstrates our desperate need for peace.

To improve our chances of finding peace, we must first find a way to sow it. We can't reap a harvest of contentment until we have first sowed the peace that we, ourselves, long for.

Much of the conflict we encounter is, unfortunately, prevalent in our familial relationships. We experience a wide variety of dysfunction in our marriages and with our immediate families. We fail to recognize the damage that resulted from long-standing sibling rivalries or the scars that remain from an abusive parent. We underestimate the physical and mental toll that this conflict has taken on us, and are blind to the barriers it creates to building healthy relationships later in life.

Making peace in these difficult situations requires us to set aside our pride and accept the fact that we may never get the apologies or reparations we feel we deserve.

In Hebrews 12:14, we learn that we should strive for peace with everyone we encounter, regardless of our differences. Though it may require a Herculean effort, finding peace brings out a holiness that will draw us closer to our savior, Jesus Christ.

MY PRAYER

God, let peace begin with me at this moment. Guide me through the challenge of extending peace and forgiveness to those who were once my enemies so that I may one day reap a harvest of righteousness and draw myself closer to You. Amen.

READ	MATTHEW 5:23-26

RESPOND

- *In what part of your life do you feel the greatest sense of dissatisfaction?*

- *In which of your unreconciled relationships are you being prompted to sow peace?*

CONTEMPLATE

- *Based on your understanding of God, explain why He wants us to sow peace where conflict exists?*

CHECK YOUR MOTIVES

You desire but do not have, so you kill. You covet but you cannot get what you want, so you quarrel and fight. You do not have because you do not ask God. When you ask, you do not receive, because you ask with wrong motives, that you may spend what you get on your pleasures. (James 4:2-3 NIV)

Have you ever wanted something so badly that you obsessed about it? Maybe it was a new truck, motorcycle or a fishing pole. Did you want it so desperately that you actually prayed for it? There are times in all our lives when our sole focus is on getting something we want.

As you begin to better understand God, you learn that He is infinitely gracious and wants us to be happy, but He does not like it when we idolize worldly possessions.

In Matthew 7:7-11, we learn that our heavenly father wants us to have the things we need. He wants us to go to Him in prayer and petition for the things we want, but He shows favor to those who approach Him with selfless prayers that are offered on behalf of others in need.

It takes a tremendous amount of discipline to discern between what we truly need and what we simply want. When we set aside our selfish desires and focus our attention on the needs of others, God rewards us with the treasure of eternal life in a place where worldly possessions have no value.

Our requests to God should be the ones where He will be glorified as a result of answering that prayer. When we pray for God to heal someone's illness and reduce another's pain, we know that praise and thanksgiving will be lavished upon Him when those prayers are answered.

When we shift our focus away from having our own needs met and ask God to answer the needs of others, we begin to more fully see the miraculous and generous God we serve.

MY PRAYER
God, turn my focus away from my own selfish needs and let me dwell on the needs of others when I come to You in prayer. You are a gracious and loving God whose grace is sufficient for every need we might ever have. Amen.

READ	PHILIPPIANS 2:1-11

RESPOND
- *Describe a worldly possession that you once obsessed about.*

- *Give an example of one of your most selfish desires.*

CONTEMPLATE
- *Based on your understanding of God's nature, why is it important that we offer prayers on behalf of others?*

FOCUS ON THE KINGDOM

You adulterous people, don't you know that friendship with the world means enmity against God? Therefore, anyone who chooses to be a friend of the world becomes an enemy of God. (James 4:4 NIV)

As men, we spend a lot of time obsessing over the latest and greatest toys at our disposal. We like our 50-inch televisions, power tools, and all-terrain vehicles. Some of us have created "man caves" in our homes where we can escape from the outside world and surround ourselves with our favorite gadgets.

Our infatuation with the things of this world speaks to the depth of our isolation and, worse yet, drives a wedge between us and God. In the end, God finds Himself competing for our attention against things that are, at best, only temporary.

These distractions have become modern-day idols for us. We get sucked into the trap of worshipping technology instead of spending time with our wives and children or in quiet time with God. We have developed a fear of intimacy in our relationships because we don't like to face the pain of our inadequacies.

We are reminded in 1 John 2:15-17 that we are not to fall in love with the things of this world. Instead, we should turn our focus to heaven and the rewards that come with eternal life.

Putting such intense focus on anything but God separates us from Him. We should, however, be encouraged by the promise of better things to come when we leave this world. In John 14:2, we are told of the mansions that await us in heaven. God wants us to be eager to join him in a perfect place where there is no sickness, poverty, pain or envy. By focusing our hopes on our eternal home, we will be more likely to serve others and lead earthly lives that will be pleasing to God.

MY PRAYER

God, help me to turn my focus away from the comforts and frivolities of this world so that I can set my eyes on the more noble goal of an eternal life with You. Nothing compares to the love You have for me or Your promise of salvation. Amen.

READ	1 JOHN 2:15-17

RESPOND

- *When you consider all of your worldly possessions, which of them bring you closer to living a life that is pleasing to God? What possessions tend to push you away from God?*

- *For what reason are worldly possessions compared to idols?*

CONTEMPLATE

- *What does eternal life look like to you?*

SET ASIDE PRIDE

But he gives us more grace. That is why Scripture says: "God opposes the proud but shows favor to the humble." Submit yourselves, then, to God. Resist the devil, and he will flee from you. (James 4:6-7 NIV)

If you learn just one thing from the Book of James, it should be that pride is the one thing most likely to harm our relationship with God and others. Our pride stems from our desire to take credit for everything we've accomplished without acknowledging God's roles in our success.

Pride is borne out of a sole focus on oneself with little regard for God or others. This self-righteousness and conceit is a sin and leads to a more destructive pattern of sin. God hates pride because it keeps us from seeking Him.

We show our pride when we are argumentative, when we insist on being right, and when we are impatient with others. Pride is the root of all sin. In Jeremiah 9:23-24, we are taught that the only thing we should ever boast about is the fact that we know and love the all-powerful God. He deserves all of the glory in the world. By embracing and practicing humility, we break down the barriers of sin and begin to restore our relationship with God.

We should strive to be transparent with God about our weaknesses and ask Him to walk with us as we work to repair the relationships that have been damaged by our pride.

When we give God credit for the work He has done in our lives, others will see that we are glorifying God by the way we live our lives. The simple act of walking with humility will open the floodgates of compassion from our creator, and we will encounter a world of endless possibilities.

MY PRAYER

God, Thank you for Your endless mercy and grace. Make me ever mindful of the destructive nature of my pride and how it separates me from You. Let me glorify You by humbly serving and loving others. Amen.

READ	GALATIANS 6:1-5

RESPOND

- *What do you believe are the causes of your pride?*

- *In what ways does your prideful nature trigger other behaviors?*

CONTEMPLATE

- *What might an increased focus on humility look like in your life? How would it influence your actions? How would it impact your relationships?*

GROW NEARER TO GOD

Come near to God and he will come near to you Wash your hands, you sinners, and purify your hearts, you double-minded. (James 4:8 NIV)

In some respects, our relationship with God should be reciprocal in nature. The more we put into the relationship, the more we're going to get out of it. Growing closer to God involves investing time to read the Word on a daily basis, studying God's nature, praying and asking God to be present in every part of our lives. Once the bond is established, we must do our part to actively nurture and grow the relationship.

Hopefully, our actions will mirror what's in our hearts. It would be hypocritical to have one foot inside the Jesus camp while the other foot stays planted in our sinful past. God is jealous, and He wants 100 percent of us.

Our motives must be pure, and our hearts should be totally committed to Him. It may not be easy modifying our thoughts and actions so that we can be closer to God but the reward is great.

The return on this investment of focus is unmatched. God is already all in. The rest is up to us. In Deuteronomy 31:6 we are encouraged to be strong and courageous knowing that God is with us at all times, never leaving or forsaking us. In exchange for this privilege, we are asked to rid our lives of sinfulness, confessing the sins we do commit and honoring God by the way we live. By living a life that is consistent, we will glorify God and set an example for those around us.

MY PRAYER

God, draw me closer to You. Help me shed my sinful ways so that I may trade my old life for an eternal life with You. Let me be steadfast in my pursuit of Your favor and blessings while reflecting a life that is transformed for Your glory. Amen.

READ	PSALM 139: 1-18

RESPOND

- *Why does God think about us so much?*

- *What part of your sinful life would be the hardest for you to give up?*

CONTEMPLATE

- *Knowing what you know about God's nature, why is it important that we become 100 percent committed to living a life that glorifies Him?*

RESIST SLANDER

Brothers and sisters, do not slander one another. Anyone who speaks against a brother or sister or judges them speaks against the law and judges it. When you judge the law, you are not keeping it, but sitting in judgment on it. There is only one Lawgiver and Judge, the one who is able to save and destroy. But you — who are you to judge your neighbor? (James 4: 11-12 NIV)

There are many references in the Bible to the sinfulness of slander, gossip, and evil thoughts about others. While the use of derogatory words may seem rather commonplace in our everyday lives, when you look at the root causes of why we speak ill words, you get a complete understanding of why this type of sin is so offensive to God.

The Ninth Commandment tells us that we shall not bear false witness against our neighbors. If slander ranks high enough on the list of sins that it was included in the Ten Commandments, God must have a particular disdain for this type of infraction. If you peel back the layers of slander and gossip, you will see that this spoken form of sin commonly involves manipulating the truth in the interest of self-glory.

In reality, we are regurgitating hate about other people for the sole intent of making ourselves look better. Our attempts to exaggerate or distort the truth are made for the unsavory purpose of positioning ourselves in a more favorable light. That is shameful, no matter how you look at it.

In Ephesians 4:29, we are told that the only words that should come from our mouths are ones that build up and give grace to other people. Corrupt words should never be spoken.

God wants us to abandon our desire to gossip, slander and speak evil of other people. Because all of us were created in His image, we can only imagine God's disappointment when we attack and criticize His beloved children.

MY PRAYER

God, let only positive words come from my mouth. Use me to build others up rather than tearing them down. Let me see all people through the lens as they were created in Your perfect image. Amen.

READ	1 PETER 3:7-12

RESPOND

- *Why are slander and gossip really about nothing more than self-glory?*

- *Why is God disappointed when we slander others?*

CONTEMPLATE

- *Write about a time when you were the victim of slander or gossip. Describe your feelings. How did you respond?*

SURRENDER CONTROL

Now listen, you who say, "Today or tomorrow we will go to this or that city, spend a year there, carry on business and make money." Why, you do not even know what will happen tomorrow. What is your life? You are a mist that appears for a little while and then vanishes. Instead, you ought to say, "If it is the Lord's will, we will live and do this or that." (James 4:13-15 NIV)

A desire to have complete control over every aspect of our lives is something that seems to be built into our DNA as men. In our everlasting search for significance, we need things to go a certain way and on a specific timeline.

The truth is that this defect is not borne out of a biological deficiency; it ultimately has much more to do with our inability to put our complete trust in God. If we can't put our complete trust in God, we might as well acknowledge the fact that we aren't going to be able to put our trust in anyone, no matter how close they may be.

God is unlimited in His power. In Proverbs 19:21 we are reminded that while man has many plans in his own mind, God's purpose and providence is what remains standing at the end of the day. Once we accept this eternal truth, we can begin to take comfort in surrendering and opening ourselves to the many wonderful things God has planned for our lives.

The good news comes in Jeremiah 29:11 as we learn that God's plans for us are for good and not evil. For that reason, we can eliminate our need for control by simply giving in and trusting God to carry out His preordained plans.

Our surrender is complicated by the fact that it's difficult to trust someone we don't really know. Therefore, we must become steadfast in our endeavors to know God better by studying His word and seeking Him in all that we do.

MY PRAYER
God, help me to see more clearly Your sovereignty so that I might completely surrender my desire for control by trusting in Your good and perfect plan for my life. Amen.

READ	ISAIAH 55:8-11

RESPOND
- *In what areas of your life do you struggle most with issues of control?*

- *What are the risks associated with putting your complete trust in someone you know and love?*

CONTEMPLATE
- *Recall a time in your life when you completely surrendered control of a given situation. How did it make you feel? What were the risks and rewards?*

REJECT PASSIVITY

If anyone, then, knows the good they ought to do and doesn't do it, it is sin for them. (James 4:17 NIV)

As men, our issues with passivity began in the Garden of Eden. Unfortunately, things have only gotten worse for us as society's expectations and popular entertainment's portrayal of men have reduced us to lazy bums, addicted to football and video games.

While this characterization is mostly unfair, God is still disappointed by our decision to lead passive lives, surrendering the initiative to lead our families, workplaces, churches, and communities.

In 2 Timothy 1:7, Paul reminds Timothy that God gifted him with the spirit of power, love, and a strong mind. We are no different. Our timidity stems from our overexposure to stimuli such as social media, video games, and pornography that steal our mental and moral vigor and replaces it with a general sense of fear, shame, and apathy.

This aimlessness has given birth to societal issues that have eroded our family structures and left our wives and children feeling abandoned. We can do better.

It's true that many of us look for any excuse to retreat from our responsibility to lead. All it takes is a critical word from our wives, and we instantly give up and say, "If you don't like the way I'm leading the family, you do it!" Man does not need to rule the earth, but men should step up and carry the largest share of the burden associated with upholding a strong moral standard and leading our families and communities in a manner that brings honor to God.

MY PRAYER

God, empower me to "man up" and take my place as the leader of my family and in my community. Help me to reject passivity by strengthening my focus and purpose on this earth. Help me to overcome the sinful lure of the things that separate me from You. Amen.

READ	JOSHUA 24: 14-15

RESPOND

- *What are the obstacles that keep you from stepping up to lead your family?*

- *In what areas of your life do you struggle most with passivity?*

CONTEMPLATE

- *Write about your family of origin. Who assumed the leadership role in your family when you were growing up? Was that person effective? Why or why not?*

GIVE GENEROUSLY

Come now, you rich, weep and howl for the miseries that are coming upon you. Your riches have rotted and your garments are moth-eaten. Your gold and silver have corroded, and their corrosion will be evidence against you and will eat your flesh like fire. You have laid up treasure in the last days. (James 5:1-3 NIV)

We live under the false pretense that a man's worth is tied to the amount of money he earns. Our quest to accumulate wealth may seem like the right thing to do, but in the end, our love of money is at the root of evil and sinfulness.

In Matthew 6:24, we learn that we cannot serve two masters because of our propensity to love one and hate the other. For that exact reason, we cannot serve both God and money. We should, however, be intentional with our financial resources, putting them to work in a way that honors God by helping those less fortunate.

The Bible has plenty to say about the cheerful givers who use their money to help others. In 2 Corinthians 9:10-11, the Apostle Paul tells us that the real reward for our generosity comes when the recipients of our generosity give praise and thanksgiving to God for providing for their needs. Even though we labored to provide for the poor, God still gets the credit. Nothing could be more perfect or appropriate. Our resources, however great or small, are gifts from a loving God.

We honor Him when we give generously, expecting nothing in return. We should feel compelled to give as if no one is watching and then find joy and comfort in the fact that God gets the glory. When you consider that our generosity is only made possible by the grace that God has extended to us, it all seems rather fitting.

MY PRAYER

God, let my heart be overcome by the desire to give generously, especially when no one is watching. May You be glorified in every act of kindness I extend to those who are in need. Amen.

READ	LUKE 21:1-4

RESPOND

- *Why does God love a cheerful giver?*

- *Why is the love of money considered to be the root of evil?*

CONTEMPLATE

- *Describe how it feels to give when no one is looking. What are the benefits associated with not being recognized for your generosity?*

BE DILIGENT

Be patient, then, brothers and sisters, until the Lord's coming. See how the farmer waits for the land to yield its valuable crop, patiently waiting for the autumn and spring rains. You too, be patient and stand firm, because the Lord's coming is near. (James 5:7-8 NIV)

To be diligent is to persist with constant effort to accomplish something worthwhile. Most of us are not diligent by nature. We represent a generation of men who have grown up in a culture of instant coffee, instant noodles, and instant energy. We want it our way right now, but we often lack the purpose and passion necessary to see a plan through from start to finish.

To make matters worse, the distractions we've created make it difficult for us to stay engaged and focused. Thankfully, we serve a God who is patient and persistent in spite of our shortcomings.

In Galatians 6:9, we are taught that our good deeds and service will yield great rewards only if we remain patient and steadfast. If you've heard the term, "Good things come to those who wait" you probably understand that the best things to come to us are usually things for which we've worked the hardest.

There is a direct correlation between our efforts and the rewards we receive. God gives us renewed assurance that we will indeed reap what we sow.

In Proverbs 21:5, we are reminded that diligence leads to abundance while haste leads to poverty. Our great hope is that our diligence will eventually bring significance and gratification to our lives. Like the farmer who waits months for the first fruits of his harvest, our lives require a similar discipline. Be diligent in all you do. The reward is close at hand.

MY PRAYER

God, give me the determination, persistence, and grit to pursue the things that will add richness to my life and depth to my relationship with You. Allow me the forbearance to carry out what You desire of me from start to finish. Amen.

READ	PROVERBS 13:4

RESPOND

- *How dependent are you on instant gratification?*

- *What do you believe is your purpose or passion in life?*

CONTEMPLATE

- *How has diligence or persistence paid off for you in your life?*

PRAY CONFIDENTLY

Is anyone among you in trouble? Let them pray. Is anyone happy? Let them sing songs of praise. Is anyone among you sick? Let them call the elders of the church to pray over them and anoint them with oil in the name of the Lord. And the prayer offered in faith will make the sick person well; the Lord will raise them up. If they have sinned, they will be forgiven. (James 5:13-15 NIV)

God loves it when we talk to Him. Our prayers can be intimate conversations with God, but we may be reluctant to go to Him in prayer because we believe our needs are unworthy of His attention. Nothing could be further from the truth. God loves hearing from us and welcomes our prayers, regardless of how simple or haphazard the delivery. Learning to add structure to your prayers will give you more confidence and make you feel at ease when going to God in prayer.

When you pray, it's best to begin by praising God and giving thanks for His unconditional love and the wonders of His universe. Secondly, you should confess your sins and ask God for forgiveness. Next, offer intercessory prayer on behalf of other people. It is important that you use this time with God to pray on behalf of others, asking that His grace and mercy be extended to those on your prayer list.

Praying for just your individual needs reveals a weakness in your faith. Lastly, you should bring your specific concerns to God. This is an excellent opportunity to pray for wisdom, healing, and guidance as you deal with issues of fear, worry and shame.

We are reminded in Luke 11:9 that when we ask God for things through prayer, our prayers are always answered. These prayers may not be answered on the timeline or manner we prefer, but we must have patience and trust God to work in whatever way He sees fit.

In the end, the answer to our prayers may not be what we wanted to hear, but we should proceed with confidence knowing that God is with us and His response is always righteous and correct.

MY PRAYER

God, teach me to pray. Let my conversations with You be a reflection of my love and respect for You and those around me. Grant me the confidence I need to be bold in my prayer life, always honoring your sovereignty and recognizing the grace and mercy you have extended in my life. Amen.

READ	MATTHEW 6:5-8

RESPOND

- *How consistent is your prayer life? How can it be improved?*

- *One's faith and confidence are often aligned. In what area of your life are you currently feeling uncertain? How might prayer help?*

CONTEMPLATE

- *Take a few moments to write out a prayer using the structure suggested above. 1) Give thanks. 2) Confess your sins and seek forgiveness. 3) Pray for others. 4) Present your needs to God.*

CONFESS YOUR SINS

Therefore confess your sins to each other and pray for each other so that you may be healed. The prayer of a righteous person is powerful and effective. (James 5:16 NIV)

There's something quite liberating about confessing our sins. If you have even the slightest bit of remorse about the sin in your life, you'll find that talking about it with God or having a conversation with a trusted friend will give you a sense of freedom and relief. The Bible makes it pretty clear that he who confesses his sin will be given mercy, and he who conceals a sin will suffer.

Confessing our sin is only the first part of the process. God wants us to take it one step further and repent from this disobedient and rebellious behavior. He's not interested in seeing us commit a sinful behavior over and over, then repeatedly seeking forgiveness for the same sin simply by confessing it.

Turning away from sin and turning toward God shows that we're truly sorrowful for our past indiscretions. God is understanding and knows that, because of our sinful nature, we may have a tendency to backslide.

Beyond confession and repentance, we are told in Matthew 5:23-24 that we should seek reconciliation with those we've sinned against before we seek forgiveness from God. That complicated act of contrition demonstrates to God that we are indeed remorseful and interested in making peace where our sins have caused hardship.

Lastly, we should not forget that our sin was paid for at the cross when Jesus was crucified, but God still wants us to pursue righteousness. Though we are forgiven, we should make every effort to make amends for our sins and then turn away from sinful behavior. Confess. Repent. Reconcile.

MY PRAYER

God, forgive me for my sins and the harm that I have caused others. Today, I repent from the sins that have driven a wedge between us. Guide me as I seek reconciliation with those I've sinned against. Amen.

READ	EPHESIANS 4: 25-32

RESPOND

- *What do you believe is the significance of confessing our sins?*

- *Which of the following steps do you find the most difficult to do? Confession, repentance or reconciliation?*

CONTEMPLATE

- *Based on your understanding of God's nature, why do you believe He was willing to exchange His son's life for the forgiveness of our sins?*

ADDITIONAL RESOURCES

FredParry.Life
Becoming The Man God Intended You To Be

Interested in using this book for a small group
or Bible Study? Visit our website for FREE study
materials, discussion questions, rules of engagement
for small group participants, and other learning aids.

Want to offer feedback? Write to Fred Parry,
711 West Broadway, Columbia, Missouri 65203
www.FredParry.Life

Walking With James: Becoming The Man God Intended You To Be is a refreshingly relevant book that touches the hearts and minds of men by helping them navigate the issues that can separate them from Christ. Based on 30 pearls of wisdom found in the Book of James, this unique combination of a Bible Study and 30-day devotional is designed to challenge men to become a better version of themselves.

"I love men whose talk and walk travel together. Fred Parry is that kind of man. God has dramatically given him a new life, inside and out. And in Fred's book, *Walking With James*, he is asking you to join him and do what he has already done many times .... gather men together, and together, drink deeply from one of the most practical books of the Bible. It was a game-changer for him, and I believe it will be for you too!"

Dr. Robert Lewis
Founder, Men's Fraternity

Fred Parry has worked as a successful magazine publisher, radio host, and television commentator who struggled through his own brokenness to find a meaningful relationship with Christ. Now a Christian writer, Fred has dedicated himself to helping men understand how the Word of God can transform their lives and empower them to develop more meaningful and fulfilling relationships with God, their families and other men.

Fred continues to work in publishing and is an elected county commissioner in Columbia, Missouri, where he lives with his wife, Melody, and college-age sons Max and Nick.

FredParry.Life
Becoming The Man God Intended You To Be

ISBN 9781642541847 $14.95
51495

9 781642 541847